From Tunisia to Christ:

Once a Muslim

JAMES JESSER

with Dr. Ahmed Joktan

FROM TUNISIA TO CHRIST

ONCE A MUSLIM

JAMES JESSER

With Dr. Ahmed Joktan

PROCLAIM PUBLISHERS

ORLANDO, FLORIDA

From Tunisia to Christ: Once a Muslim

ISBN: 978-1-954858-62-6   eBook
978-1-954858-60-2   Paperback
978-1-954858-61-9   Hardback

Proclaim Publishers
1317 Edgewater Drive, Suite 4774, Orlando, Florida, 32804
proclaimpublishers.com

First Printing: August 2025
Manufactured in the United States of America

"God is the desire of every human being, whether they are aware of this fact or not."

I thank God for this opportunity to share the goodness of what He has done in my life. I am hopeful for how He will use this testimony to help others. It is my prayer that this book touches hearts and opens eyes to see the truth.

I dedicate this book to my pastor, Gordon John Manché, and to all my brothers and sisters in Christ.

TABLE OF CONTENTS

FOREWORD

This is the story of a Tunisian man's journey from a devout Muslim to a fervent Christian. It is a narrative that unfolds through internal struggle, self-discovery, and ultimately a radical shift in faith. The author, Jesser, recounts his life, detailing the deep-rooted beliefs he inherited, the questions that began to plague him, and the revelations that led him to embrace Christianity.

Born into a Muslim family like myself, Jesser's early life was steeped in Islamic traditions. He diligently read the Quran, found solace in the company of his Sufi grandfather, and enjoyed sermons by renowned imams (preachers). And yet, even in his youthful zeal, Jesser felt a dissonance between his beliefs and the realities he witnessed. He questioned the government's suppression of religious expression and the perceived injustices inflicted upon Muslims by Western powers.

At the age of fifteen, Jesser embraced a rebellious phase, aligning himself with like-minded individuals who felt a disconnect from societal norms. Their motto, "the end justifies the means," fueled their pursuit of a "quick buck," leading them to contemplate illegal acts such as bank robbery and hacking. However, a seemingly trivial event - the theft of an Italian catechism book - inadvertently sparked a new phase in Jesser's journey.

Three years later, after transferring to a private school, Jesser found himself inadvertently drawn to Christianity. He claimed to be a Christian, captivating his classmates with a fabricated tale of a Christian upbringing in Italy. This self-imposed deception forced him to delve into Christian Scriptures, searching for answers to the questions he encountered.

Jesser's exploration was fueled by a combination of genuine curiosity and a need to maintain his fabricated persona. He discovered a newfound respect for Christianity, particularly after encountering the Sermon on the Mount. However, Jesser grappled with the contradictions between Jesus' teachings and the Islamic doctrine. He questioned the validity of the Quran in the face of verses that appeared to contradict each other, and he struggled to reconcile the Islamic emphasis on obedience with the Christian concept of a loving and merciful God.

The author's journey further intensified with his discovery of the Quran's textual discrepancies and the implications of its collection process. He questioned the notion of a divinely protected text, particularly given the existence of different Quranic readings and interpretations. He felt deeply troubled by the verses regarding slavery and the limitations imposed upon women within Islam, finding them to be unjust and at odds with his evolving understanding of God's character.

Jesser's search for answers led him to a deeper appreciation for the Bible, particularly the Old Testament. He saw Jesus as the fulfillment of the promises and prophecies found in the earlier Scriptures, culminating in the ultimate sacrifice for humanity. He found solace in the Christian narrative of a loving and forgiving God, a God who seeks a personal relationship with His followers.

The author's conversion to Christianity was a turning point, bringing him both joy and persecution. He embraced his new faith with fervor, sharing his newfound beliefs with anyone who would listen. This resulted in alienation from family and friends, forcing him to find refuge in a supportive community of fellow believers.

Jesser concludes his narrative by reflecting on the tumultuous events of the Tunisian Revolution, a time of profound upheaval marked by escalating violence and religious extremism. He observes the contradictory nature of Islam, highlighting the violent verses used to justify acts of terror, while acknowledging the presence of verses advocating peace and tolerance.

Jesser's story serves as a powerful testament to the transformative power of faith and the ongoing struggle for truth. It challenges readers to question their own beliefs, consider alternative perspectives, and embrace a God of love and forgiveness.

Dr. Ahmed Joktan

December 24, 2024

CHAPTER 1: CATECHISMO

"The end justifies the means."

I lived in Tunisia, a country that is mentioned in the Bible as Tarshish, the place where the prophet Jonah had planned to go instead of going to Nineveh. It is where the Old and New Testaments were collected during the Third Council of Carthage (397 A.D.). Tunisia is also the hometown of St. Augustin, St. Cyprian, and thousands of Christian martyrs whose blood was shed for their faith.

In 661 A.D., following six battles, the once holy grounds of Tunisia were seized, and the place where Mediterranean powers, bishops, and elders of the early churches used to gather was captured. The conversations of biblical doctrines were crying out for those with ears to hear.

As a result of the invasion, Tunisia became a Muslim country. Nevertheless, the Tunisian people could not fully assimilate to the culture brought by this new religion, and consequently, they created a melting pot, incorporating both the old and new cultures. Today, even after the Arab Spring, Tunisia is known for being one of the least religious and most tolerant of all Muslim countries.

As for me, I was born into a typical Tunisian family. My father was a physical education teacher and my mother was a primary school teacher.

Together, they raised my little sister and me. My birth date holds quite a religious significance. I was born on April 12th, 1991, a day that coincided with Friday (the holiest day of the week for Muslims) on the 27th of Ramadan (known as Layat al-Qadr, "The night of power"). It is the holiest day of the holiest month on the Islamic calendar. Hence, my family thought it would be only convenient to name me "Mohamed". My father eventually decided against it, and I was named "Jesser" ("bold and courageous" in Arabic).

Growing up, I was religious. I loved reading the Quran daily, although I did not quite understand it. I also found a lot of pleasure in my grandfather's company. He was a spiritual man, a Sufi, which is a smaller sect of Islam. I extensively watched sermons by various Muslim preachers, such as Amro Khaled, Zaghloul Ennajjar, Sheikh Hassen, and Wajdi Ghnim, to name a few. I thoroughly enjoyed listening to the Quran as it was recited by Abdurrahman Assudaisi and Alaafasi, both of whom were professionals in the Tartil (a way to read the Quran melodically).

Even though I was fairly zealous, I was never able to be a fully committed Muslim. I was against the government and the dictatorship of the ex-president, whom I perceived as the devil's tool since he was always trying to keep us from obeying God. The government persecuted those who tried to openly practice their religious beliefs, fearing the possibility of extremists who would become a threat to the sovereignty of the state.

As a Muslim, I believed being separated from religion was the main reason behind the devolution of Muslim nations. I believed the conspiracy that the prominent enemies from the West, most notably the United States and Israel, were holding back true Muslims from walking in the holiness of the Sharia Law. By following this law, Muslims are in obedience to all of God's laws and commandments. I had hoped to see the Muslim people freed from oppressive regimes so that Islam would rule the world.

At the age of fifteen, I spent a lot of time with like-minded, rebellious people. We were constantly thinking about how to make a quick and easy buck. We considered robbing a bank or becoming hackers. Our motto was, "the end justifies the means". At that time, I believed our mischievous plots to be fully justified; since we wanted to rob the evil government, it would be considered Halal (religiously legal). I yearned to be a thief, just like my childhood hero, Robin Hood; it would be a boyhood dream turned into reality.

During a weekly visit to the city market, I stumbled upon a toy shop, which shortly thereafter became a favorite of mine. I had childlike joy perusing the toys, looking for Pokémon and Avatar characters. Among the assortment, an Italian book caught my attention. The book was titled *Catechismo Della Chiesa Cattolica*.

Inside were several pictures depicting Jesus, churches, and saints. I felt that there was something special about the book, and I wanted to buy it. I did not have enough money, so I managed to tuck the book into my backpack and successfully smuggle it out of the store. I had no idea why I took the book, as I was neither a Christian nor spoke Italian, but I was intrigued.

Three years passed, and I transferred to a private school in a different city. My mother had to make many budget cuts to afford the school fees but she wanted to provide me with the best education possible. It was quite hard for me to fit in at first, so I mostly kept to myself. I played the drums in a metal band, wore black shirts, and grew out my hair. My look was a little unusual and culturally unacceptable, but my hoodies and earphones made hiding a lot easier.

There was a particular school day when everything changed. I found myself in the classroom with my schoolmates, waiting for a teacher who never came. Everyone else was talking with each other while I sat in the back of the classroom, listening to my heavy metal music and drumming on the desk with two pens. I became bored and decided to look for something else to do.

While searching in my bag for something to read, I found the Italian book that I had stolen three years prior. By this time, I had fortunately learned some Italian. I decided to give the book a try, thinking to myself, *let's discover what those Christians believe!*

As I was reading, my classmates began eyeing me. One of them approached and said, "What do you have there? You're *reading*? Don't get too excited now!", the sarcasm in his words tangible.

I composedly lifted my eyes and said, "Well, I am reading the Bible." I could see the confusion in his expression.

"What does Bible mean?" he asked.

I turned the book over and said, "Enjil" (Gospel, in Arabic). My classmate smiled and said, "That sounds really interesting, but as far as I know, that book is for Christians. So why are *you* reading it?"

My response to this question came without forethought: "Well, simply, because I am Christian."

A deafening silence fell over the entire classroom. Everyone was giving me bewildered stares, as though I were an extraterrestrial. The silence was eventually broken with another question.

"You are Tunisian. How can you be Christian?"

I was in too deep to back down at that point, so I told my classmates fabrications I had never said in my life. I told them that I came from a Tunisian father but an Italian mother and that I had lived in Italy for five years. I said that my real name was changed from "James" to "Jesser" because it is illegal in Tunisia to have a non-Arabic name. And because I was raised by a Christian mother, it was only natural for me to be a Christian. My tale was the product of an overactive imagination and I told it purely for self-amusement, but the entire class became convinced.

My classmates could not fathom my proclamation; they started making detailed queries about my beliefs and the differences between Christianity and Islam. I found myself in an awkward situation; I had no understanding of Christian precepts or nuances of the faith. Simultaneously, I did not want my classmates to know I lied. So, to elude answering their multitudinous inquiries, I told them that I would give them all answers in a week.

I was headed home when I came across an atheist from my neighborhood. Despite believing that no God exists, this man knew about many religions. I asked him if he had any information about Christianity. He provided some keywords and said to search the internet to find out more. That evening, I started searching online for the basics of

Christianity and managed to obtain some useful information to further convince my classmates that I was a bona fide Christian believer.

CHAPTER 2: THE DILEMMA

"Its words created a great dilemma for me... so beautiful and true, but it was as though it was written to the Muslims."

I had a small radio which kept me company while doing my homework, and the folkloric tunes helped lull me to sleep at night. One night, I was trying to tune my radio to a Romanian station but found something different. Amid the static, I discovered a Christian radio station in Arabic. I had never heard of Arab Christians before! The preacher was talking about the Sermon on the Mount from the book of Matthew in the Christian Bible. The teachings were incredible!

My knowledge of Islam was similar to that of most Muslims. I believed Jesus was a prophet, like Moses and Abraham. I believed He was sent to the Jews with the Gospel (Enjil) because they corrupted the Torah and strayed far from the right path. From my understanding, Jesus was born from a virgin. During His lifetime, He performed many miracles by God's power. He foretold the coming of the last prophet, Mohamed. The Jews opposed Jesus' teachings and wanted to kill Him. However, He was raptured by God. Judas, the one who betrayed Him, was crucified instead. The Christians had corrupted the books of Jesus by writing different versions of the Gospel. In the corrupted versions, Christians were allowed to drink alcohol, eat pork, and have pre-marital sex.

Many Muslims believe that the corrupted Gospel asserts Jesus as the offspring of a sexual relationship between Mary and God[1]. Hence, there were three gods instead of one. Therefore, God sent the prophet Mohamed with a new, incorruptible book known as the Quran. The Quran was to destroy the aforementioned heresies, setting people straight. *

As I listened to the man preaching on the radio station, my curiosity was piqued. I was surprised that it is written in the Enjil that sexual immorality is a sin. I was intrigued to learn that Christians have only one book, the Holy Bible. The preacher spoke about the Bible and how it contains the Old Testament, which includes the Torah and the books of the prophets who came before Jesus, i.e., David, Solomon, Jonah, etc. I learned the Bible also contains the New Testament, which describes prayer and fasting. It heightened my curiosity to gain further insight about Christians.

Therefore, every Thursday night, I tuned my small radio to this broadcast. I would write the

---

[1] Al-Jinn 72:3; Al-An'am 6:101; "Collyridianism," *Wikipedia*, last modified June 10, 2025, https://en.wikipedia.org/wiki/Collyridianism.

verses of the Bible that were mentioned in the program and memorized them. Muslims are encouraged to memorize the Quran, so I wanted to be ready in case my classmates asked me if I was memorizing the Scriptures.

In reading the Scriptures, I came across the Sermon on the Mount again. Its words created a great dilemma for me. The sermon was so beautiful and true, but it was as though it was written to the Muslims. I wavered between my belief in the Quran and the Bible's words of Jesus: "For most certainly, I tell you, until heaven and earth pass away, not even one smallest letter or one tiny pen stroke shall in any way pass away from the law, until all things are accomplished" (Matthew 5:18). I agreed with this verse because God is omnipotent and no one can change His words. However, Muslims believe that the old books were changed. I wondered how God was not able to protect His word. If the Muslims were right and the word of God was indeed changed, it would mean God was not able to save His word; He could not have kept His promise to preserve it.

From my understanding, Christians read the Torah and the books of the old prophets believing nothing changed and added books to the Bible, which they use in their ceremonies. Even though

Jews do not believe in Jesus as their Messiah, they read from the same Torah as the Christians.

I wondered - if the Torah was corrupted, was it corrupted before Christianity or after Christianity began? If before, then why do the Christians believe in the Torah? If the Torah was corrupted after the coming of Jesus, would it have been possible for the Christians and the Jews to agree to change it? But that did not make sense, as the first Christians were persecuted by the Jews.

In Matthew 5:31-32 of the Sermon on the Mount, Jesus said:

> It was also said, "Whoever shall put away his wife, let him give her a writing of divorce," but I tell you that whoever puts away his wife, except for the cause of sexual immorality, makes her an adulteress; and whoever marries her when she is put away commits adultery.

I understood these verses because I believed that God hates separation. It would be better for a husband and wife to find a solution for their issues by walking in love and forgiving each other, keeping the family together and the children from hurt. In Islam, divorce is easy; you simply tell your partner that she is divorced. So, I thought, why has God changed that? This change is not good.

In verses 38-42 of that same chapter, Jesus said thus:

> You have heard that it was said, "An eye for an eye, and a tooth for a tooth." But I tell you, don't resist him who is evil; but whoever strikes you on your right cheek, turn to him the other also. If anyone sues you to take away your coat, let him have your cloak also. Whoever compels you to go one mile, go with him two. Give to him who asks you, and don't turn away him who desires to borrow from you. (Matthew 5:38-42)

These verses show the goodness of God, and how to be peacemakers in this world. I could see the need for this teaching in my nation, because I believed that an eye for an eye only makes the whole world blind. In the Quran, it is written, "Eye for eye, and tooth for tooth" (Al-Ma'idah 5:45). It is also written: "So whoever has assaulted you, then assault him in the same way that he has assaulted you. And fear Allah and know that Allah is with those who fear Him" (Al-Baqarah 2:194).

In Matthew 5:43-48, Jesus said thus:

> You have heard that it was said, "You shall love your neighbour and hate your enemy." But I tell you, love your enemies, bless those who curse you, do good to those who

hate you, and pray for those who mistreat you and persecute you, that you may be children of your Father who is in heaven. For he makes his sun to rise on the evil and the good, and sends rain on the just and the unjust. For if you love those who love you, what reward do you have? Don't even the tax collectors do the same? If you only greet your friends, what more do you do than others? Don't even the tax collectors do the same? Therefore you shall be perfect, just as your Father in heaven is perfect.

I was overwhelmed when I heard these verses. I questioned why God changed His mind in the Quran:

Fight those who do not believe in Allah or in the Last Day and who do not consider unlawful what Allah and His Messenger have made unlawful and who do not adopt the religion of truth from those who were given the Scripture - [fight] until they give the jizyah (tax for non-believers) willingly while they are humbled. (At-Tawbah 9:29)

In Matthew 6, Jesus said the following:

When you pray, you shall not be as the hypocrites, for they love to stand and pray in the synagogues and in the corners of the streets, that they may be seen by men.

> Most certainly, I tell you, they have received their reward. But you, when you pray, enter into your inner room, and having shut your door, pray to your Father who is in secret; and your Father who sees in secret will reward you openly. In praying, don't use vain repetitions as the Gentiles do; for they think that they will be heard for their much speaking. Therefore don't be like them, for your Father knows what things you need before you ask him. (Matthew 6:5-8)

That is how I thought prayer should be. But Muslims pray in direct contrast to these words: Muslims pray standing in the streets every Friday, babble and repeat prayers, and iterate the "Fatiha", which is the first Surah (chapter) in the Quran, almost seventeen times a day.

In verses 16-18 of the same chapter, Jesus said this:

> Moreover when you fast, don't be like the hypocrites, with sad faces. For they disfigure their faces that they may be seen by men to be fasting. Most certainly I tell you, they have received their reward. But you, when you fast, anoint your head and wash your face, so that you are not seen by men to be fasting, but by your Father who

is in secret; and your Father, who sees in
secret, will reward you. (Matthew 6:16-18)

Upon reading this, I thought that Jesus must have
been here for the last Ramadan and was
commenting on what He'd seen!

Even still, it was the next few verses that
confused me the most, as Jesus was speaking about
true and false prophets:

Beware of false prophets, who come to you
in sheep's clothing, but inwardly are
ravening wolves. By their fruits you will
know them. Do you gather grapes from
thorns or figs from thistles? Even so, every
good tree produces good fruit, but the
corrupt tree produces evil fruit. A good tree
can't produce evil fruit, neither can a
corrupt tree produce good fruit. Every tree
that doesn't grow good fruit is cut down
and thrown into the fire. Therefore by their
fruits you will know them. (Matthew 7:15-
20)

By their fruits you will know them... it was evident
to me that a Muslim nation bears the fruit of
corruption, injustice, poverty, and violence.

All my questioning brought internal conflict, and
I asked God to forgive me for doubting in my heart.
Doubting and questioning are sins in Islam — "O you
who have believed, do not ask about things which,

if they are shown to you, will distress you" (Al-Ma'idah 5:101). I decided to read the Quran in a deeper way, to refuse the temptation to doubt, and to find answers to the questions. In fact, I began to study both religions, but I had no intention of changing my beliefs. Rather, I began to view Christianity in a kinder light.

CHAPTER 3: QUESTIONING

"Was God speaking to me, pushing me toward something? Or was it the devil wanting me to go to hell...?"

I was rehearsing with my band one day when I noticed the singer was wearing a necklace with a cross, though he wasn't a Christian. I asked him to let me borrow it, as I wanted to "look more Christian" to my classmates. He refused but told me there was a shop in the capital city that sells crosses; if I wanted, I could give him ten dinars and he'd buy me one. Instead of this, I told him I would visit him the following Saturday so he could show me the place and I'd make the purchase.

Next Saturday came but I was unable to make it. I therefore decided to visit the shop alone on the day of the weekly market. The bus stop was next to my favorite toy shop where I had found the *Catechismo* book. While I was looking for the cross necklaces, I happened upon a small, gray box. Removing the lid, I discovered it was full of crosses of assorted sizes and metals. There were big crosses, small crosses, golden crosses, and silver crosses! I asked the seller, "How much?"

"It's one dinar," he said. I purchased the box and returned home, full of joy!

Soon afterward, I went with my mother to the market. While visiting a shop to find my sister an alarm clock, I noticed a bookshop next door. I entered the bookshop alone and discovered a two-volume bookset written in French titled, *La Foi Chretienne* ("The Christian Faith"). Unfortunately, both books were around four dinars, which I could not afford. I was thinking of stealing them, but they were big and it would be too obvious. Instead, I opted to purchase just the first of the two volumes.

As my mother and I were walking back to the car, she asked me what I bought in the bookshop; I told her it was a book on technology. It was then I noticed that I had left my sister's clock behind in my excitement over my new book. I retrieved the clock alone from the shop; upon returning to the car, I saw my mother reading *La Foi Chretienne*. She looked at me and asked, "This is a book about technology?"

I confessed. "Well, Mom, it's a Christian book. I just didn't want to tell you because I wanted to avoid your questions."

She read a bit more, then told me, "That looks like a really amazing book."

I decided then to tell her there were two books, but since I did not have enough money, I bought only one. She gave me two dinars and asked me to buy the second volume.

Back in my room, I opened the Italian book, the box of crosses, and the two French Christian books, placing them all on my bed. While contemplating how to proceed, my mother unexpectedly appeared at my doorway and saw my Christian collection. At first, she became defensive and shouted at me; after she'd calmed down a bit, she instructed me to focus on my studies instead of wasting my time on those "stupid things". Once I tricked her into thinking they were required items for my philosophy courses, however, she let the argument go.

Surprisingly, before she walked out, my mother's tone and look changed as she said to me, "Do you know something, Jess? I actually like the Christians, so much; they look so humble. Even when I was young, my preferred singers were the Arabic Christians Majda Al-Rumi, Julia Botross, and Fayruz. My name, Nadia, was given to me by a Christian nurse who was a nun. And I don't know why, but I have always felt like they have something special—they have this peace about them. When I think of the prophets, I like Jesus the most, even more than Mohamed. To this day, I wonder why Jesus will return at the end of days and not Mohamed. And why is there an antichrist and not an anti-Mohamed?" And just like that, my mother left the room.

Her words lingered in my mind. I was feeling and thinking the same things she did but didn't have the courage to voice them. I wondered if all these occurrences were coincidental. Was God speaking to me, pushing me toward something? Or was it the devil wanting me to go to hell, bringing me all these distractions to deceive me?

I chose in this moment of questioning to repeat to myself that the Bible was corrupted, based on a lie, and a stolen book, all of which are sins. This meant I was in sin and had opened the door for the devil to destroy my faith! I therefore begged for God's forgiveness for this grievance and resolved to be more committed in my daily prayers.

CHAPTER 4: THE QURAN, THE COMMENTARIES, & THE HADITHS

*"This begs the question: has the Message been
corrupted, or is it trustworthy?"*

Along with my revived devotion to prayer, I
started reading the Quran daily with the
assistance of commentaries. There are a variety of
Quranic commentaries, such as those written by
Tabari, Kortobi, Ibn-Kathir, and Al-Jalalayn. The
Quran was written poetically in the old Arabic
language, which was far from my dialect; the
commentaries helped me to understand the
meaning of the words and verses within their
contexts. There is also no logical or chronological
order in the Quran like there is in the Bible[2], so I
needed the verses explained to better understand
their meaning.

The Quran

I learned that the Quran was written over a
period of twenty-three years in two different places:

---

[2] "Chronological Order of the Qur'an," *WikiIslam*, last modified May 19,
2025, https://wikiislam.net/wiki/Chronological_Order_of_the_Qur%27an.

Makkah (Mecca) and Medina[3]. Some of the writings were recorded on animal skins, rocks, and palm branches.

I discovered the Quran wasn't collected in the days of Mohamed; in fact, the book didn't exist at all until after Mohamed died, and then it was collected twice. The first time was during the dynasty of Al-Khalifa Abu-Bakr Al-Seddik. This first collection was later burned. The second time was in the dynasty of Al-Khalifa Othman Ibn-Affan[4].

This made me wonder: if the Quran originated with the prophet Mohamed, why didn't he have it written down during his lifetime? Muslims also believe that all the great disciples, the wives of the prophet, and the prophet himself could recite all of the Quran; this belief meant that the Quran would be hard to be changed or corrupted ("tahrif" = a corruption of the word of God), because its entirety was known during Mohamed's life and many could recite it as a whole. But as it took a long time to gather all portions of the Quran, because various disciples only knew, or at least gave, parts of it, it casts suspicion on the claim that all his great disciples knew all contents before Mohamed died.

---

[3] "Textual History of the Qur'an," *WikiIslam*, last modified May 30, 2025, https://wikiislam.net/wiki/Textual_History_of_the_Qur%27an.

[4] "Textual History of the"

Another cause for concern: the first copies of the Quran were not punctuated or had vowelization[5]. This is a critical detail because a change in one dot can change the meaning of an entire sentence in Arabic. This also means that the order of the Quran, the names of its chapters (Surahs), and the numeration of the verses were added later and not directly dictated by God to Mohamed. The addition of chapter names and verse numbers wouldn't inherently be a problem (this was done with the Christian Bible to make it easier to locate verses), except that the Quran is believed to be 100%, word for word, all of God's instruction through Mohamed;[6] instead of Mohamed being like a witness to an event describing what he heard or saw, like the writers Matthew and John were in the Bible's New Testament, Mohamed is believed to have been like a radio antenna, robot, or mouthpiece that only said the exact word-by-word phrases that God said to him.

The Muslims further believe that the Quran is in God's presence in another holy book called "Al-Laoh Al-Mahfudh" (the preserved book which is in heaven). Muslims believe the verses in the Quran on

---

[5] "Qur'anic punctuation," *Wikipedia*, last modified July 18, 2025,
https://en.wikipedia.org/wiki/Qur%27anic_punctuation.

[6] "Qur'an," *WikiIslam*, last modified March 28, 2025,
https://wikiislam.net/wiki/Qur'an.

earth and in Al-Laoh Al-Mahfudh in heaven are completely identical. But how can we be sure of that when vowelization was added by someone other than Mohamed, decades posthumously? Abu Al-Asouad Al-Douali furnished the Quran with punctuation nearly forty years after the death of Mohamed, during the dynasty of the Umayyads, because confusion had set in when Muslims started reading the Quran with completely different phrasing[7]. Therefore, the prophet never saw the book, nor was it double-checked by him, and the Quran was added to by a man other than God's prophet.

There is further evidence of outside influences in the Quran's content when one looks into phrases such as "Al-Basmala" and the unknown phrases written at the start of several Surahs. The Quran describes itself as being solely written in Arabic, e.g., "Indeed, we have sent it down as an Arabic Qur'an that you might understand" (Yusuf 12:2). And yet I found many words in the Quran that are not Arabic but have Hebrew, Aramaic, or Syriac (a dialect of Aramaic) roots or meanings. For example, "Al-Basmala" (pronounced in Arabic as "Besm Allah Ar-Rahman Ar-Rahim", which translates in English to "In the name of Allah") that is written at the start of

---

[7] "Qur'anic Punctuation"

each Surah and must be spoken before reading any portion of the Quran aloud, has a Syriac origin. Syriac Christian priests used to say this to one another (pronounced in Syriac as "Beshm iloho Rahmano Rahimo") when they sent letters to each other[8],[9].

Of the unknown words to an Arabic reader written in the Quran, here are a few examples:

- Al-Hur Al-Ain (Al-Waqiah 56:20-23) — this phrase is explained as beautiful, virgin girls in heaven. But in the Syriac dialect, it means "white grapes", which frankly makes more sense in the context of these verses, which are describing paradise: "And fruit of what they select, And the meat of fowl, from whatever they desire. And [for them are] fair women with large, [beautiful] eyes, the likenesses of pearls well-protected". Given the content before (and after verses 20-23 as well), it is more logical for it to say, "and white grapes, the likeness of pearls well protected".

---

[8] "البسملة الأنطاكية السريانية التى يستعملها الإسلام,", *Al-Kalema*, accessed August 8, 2025, https://www.alkalema.net/allah/allah49.htm.

[9] "Pre-Islamic Arab Religion in Islam," *WikiIslam*, last modified June 29, 2025, https://wikiislam.net/wiki/Pre-Islamic_Arab_Religion_in_Islam#The_Basmala.

- ◆ "Forqan" is another word for Quran, and yet it does not have a proper meaning in Arabic. However, in Syriac it means "Salvation"[10].

- ◆ Alif-Lam-Meem — these are the first letters of a number of chapters in the Quran, i.e., Surahs 2, 3, & 29-32. Arabic-speaking Muslims still do not know its meaning[11]. However, in Hebrew, it means "listen carefully". In the Surah Al-Baqarah, it states, "Alif, Lam, Meem, This is the Book about which there is no doubt, a guidance for those conscious of Allah" (Al-Baqarah 2:1-2). Rather than using words of unknown meaning, it makes far more sense if the verse is read with the Hebrew translation: "Listen carefully, This is the Book about which there is no doubt, a guidance for those conscious of Allah".

There are many other examples—too many to mention in this book. But this was enough to cause

---

[10] "القرآن - تسمية سريانية مسيحية لكتاب التذكير," *Linga*, accessed August 8, 2025, https://www.linga.org/varities-articles/MTAzOTU.

[11] "Huruf Muqatta'at (Disjointed Letters in the Qur'an)," *WikiIslam*, last modified August 3, 2024, https://wikiislam.net/wiki/Huruf_Muqatta%27at_(Disjointed_Letters_in_the_Qur%27an).

me to question the Quran and the people who explain it.

I felt that Muslims were in big trouble, as well as those who deceived the Muslim people. And all of these details led me to think, "But God promised to protect His book! After all, He said, 'We have, without doubt, sent down the Message; and we will assuredly guard it from corruption'" (Al-Hijr 15:9). Also, "The Message", or "the Book", in Arabic is "al-thekr", which is used in the Quran to describe the Quranic text, the Jewish Torah, and the Christian Enjil (Ahl Al-Thekr = the People of the Book, "the People" referring to the Jews and the Christians)[12]. And yet, Muslims are taught to believe that the Jewish and Christian texts are corrupt and cannot be trusted.

This begs the question: has the Message been corrupted, or is it trustworthy? If the Quran is trustworthy and the Quran indicates that its Message is the same as those of the Torah and Enjil, wouldn't that mean that those faiths' Scriptures were also trustworthy? And if the Message has been compromised, why didn't God protect it from corruption, as He promised to do?

---

[12] "People of the Book," *WikiIslam*, last modified June 11, 2024, https://wikiislam.net/wiki/People_of_the_Book.

The Commentaries

Moreover, there is not a singular version of the Quran, as one would think given the aforementioned Muslim belief that Mohamed was God's radio antenna and only gave completely precise, word for word transmittance of God's instructions. Currently, there are ten different "Qiraat" ("recitations" or versions) of the Quran, each with two renditions[13] (listed here by author name followed by their renditions):

1) Nafaa Al-Madani
   a. Qaloon   b. Warsh
2) Ibn-Kathir
   a. Al-Bazi   b. Qanbal
3) Abi Amro Al-Basari
   a. Al-Daori   b. Al-Sussi
4) Ibn-Amer Al-Shami
   a. Hisham   b. Ibn-Dhakouan
5) Asem Al-Kufi
   a. Shooba   b. Hafs
6) Hamza Al-Kufi
   a. Khalaf Ibn-Hisham Al-Baghdadi
   b. Khalled Ibn-Khaled

---

[13] "Textual History of the," https://wikiislam.net/wiki/Textual_History_of_the_Qur%27an#The_Qira'at_(Variant_Oral_Readings_of_the_Qur'an).

7) Al-Kasani
   a. Abu Al-Harith Al-Laith
   b. Hafs Ben Omar Al-Daori
8) Abi Jaafar Al-Madani
   a. Issa Ibn-Ouardan Al-Madani
   b. Ibn-Jammaz
9) Yaaqub Al-Khadhrami
   a. Rouis   b. Ruh Ibn-Abd Al-Moomen
10)   Khalaf Al-Aasher
   a. Ishaq Ibn-Ibrahim
   b. Idris Ibn-Abd Al-Karim Al-Hadad

Of these, most Muslims are only familiar with
a few versions[14]:

- Asem Al-Kufi's rendition "Hafs" (5b)
- Nafaa Al-Madani's two renditions "Qaloon"
  and "Warsh" (1a & 1b; used more in
  Northern Africa)
- Abi Amro Al-Basari's rendition "Al-Daori"
  (3a)

However, the existence of the ten Qiraat are known
by all students and teachers of the Sharia Law[15].
How can scholars of the Quran justify that

---

[14] See footnote 13.
[15] See footnote 13.

Mohamed gave a precise, word-for-word conveyance of God's instruction and yet twenty renditions exist?

Among these Qiraat, I was finding many differences in the Quran, and my faith was being shaken. Below are some examples:

- Ali 'Imran 3:146
  - o Hafs - وكَأَيْنْ مِنْ نبِيٍّ قَاتَلَ = fought
  - o Qaloon - وكَأَيْنْ مِنْ نبِىٍ قُتِلَ = was killed
- Ali 'Imran 3:161
  - o Hafs - وَمَا كَانَ لِنبِيٍّ أَنْ يغُلَّ = betray
  - o Qaloon - وَمَا كَانَ لِنبِىٍ أَنْ يغُلَّ = be betrayed
- Al-Baqarah 2:285
  - o Hafs- كُلٌّ آمَنَ بِاللهِ وَمَلاَئِكَتهِ وكُتبِهِ = his books
  - o Khalaf - كُلٌّ آمَنَ بِاللهِ وَمَلاَئكَتهِ وكُتِابهِ = his writers
- Al-Hujurat 49:6
  - o Hafs - يَا أَيُّهَا الَّذِينَ آمَنُوا إِنْ جَاءَكُمْ فَاسِقٌ بِنبَإٍ فَتبَيَّنُوا = investigate
  - o Qaloon - يَا أَيُّهَا الَّذِينَ آمَنُوا إِنْ جَاءَكُمْ فَاسقٌ بِنبَإٍ فَتثْبتوا = to ascertain

As seen above, words with different meanings are used across the Qiraat, which is to be considered as "Tahrif Lafdhi" (falsification in the letter)! In Surah An-Nisa, the Quran states, "Then do they not reflect upon the Qur'an? If it had been from [any] other than Allah, they would have found within it much contradiction" (An-Nisa 4:82). And yet, contradictions abound!

Additionally, which specific verses are written in Al-Laoh Al-Mahfudh, that heavenly book? There is a verse in the Quran that says, "We do not abrogate a verse or cause it to be forgotten except that We bring forth [one] better than it or similar to it" (Al-Baqarah 2:106). If God wanted to make changes, why didn't He clarify what the right or best words were instead of allowing twenty renditions to exist? Why not make the inferior phrasings be forgotten as it says in the second chapter of the Quran? And why would there be words that are unintelligible to an Arabic reader in a book that claims to be fully Arabic, but that could be understood by a Hebrew, Aramaic, or Syriac reader?

The Hadiths

I also delved into the Hadiths—the sayings of Mohamed which are not in the Quran—and therein found details that raised concern regarding their reliability as well. To start, many Muslims say the Hadiths are not handed down from God as the Quran is, believing that the writers were human and able to make mistakes. And yet, Muslims use statements from the Hadiths and the Quran with equal weight to justify their actions. But how can we trust the Hadiths or give them the same authority as the Quran if we consider one to be perfect and from God, while the other is written by imperfect men?

Looking into a particular Hadith, "Sahih Al-Bukhari" (the most trusted book after the Quran for Sunni Muslims), the author, Al-Bukhari, was from Uzbekistan and did not speak Arabic[16]. Given that a Hadith, by definition, is a collection of the sayings of Mohamed (not the word-by-word instructions from God like in the Quran but from Mohamed's conversations), this means that any phrases Al-Bukhari heard would have been translated from Arabic to his native tongue for him to understand them; as we all know, things are never quite the same when they are translated, and some of the meaning can be lost.

What's more, Al-Bukhari was born almost 200 years after the death of the prophet Mohamed. This means Mohamed's sayings passed through many generations of people before they were heard by Al-Bukhari, bringing into question how accurate all those people's memories were! Even worse, the oldest surviving copy of his book, which is not the

---

[16] "Sahih Bukhari," *WikiIslam*, last modified March 8, 2021, https://wikiislam.net/wiki/Sahih_Bukhari.

original, was written 240 years after Al-Bukhari's death, making the total gap between this Hadith and Mohamed's demise to be 440 years!

Sahih Al-Bukhari also has 7,500 Hadiths which Al-Bukhari chose out of hundreds of thousands of Mohamed's sayings. (Quick clarification: the word Hadith is used both to refer to a collection/book of the prophet's sayings as well as each of Mohamed's individual statements). These Hadiths were reportedly written in sixteen short years, meaning that Al-Bukhari had to write 102 Hadiths per day! Mathematically, this doesn't add up when you think about the author having to sleep, eat, pray five times daily, and travel to meet those who were helping him collect the Hadiths.

I decided to continue reading carefully, holding fast to the belief that God would satisfy all my concerns and questions.

CHAPTER 5: IMPURITY

"I found other injustices toward women as delineated in Islam..."

As I mentioned previously, Tunisia was not a very religious country during my upbringing. Even today, despite the onset of the Arab Spring, the Tunisian women are very strong and educated, there isn't polygamy, and the age of marriage begins at eighteen years of age. Unfortunately, barbaric laws are still applicable today in several other Muslim countries concerning women (e.g., Afghanistan, Pakistan, Saudi Arabia, and Egypt).

Regarding polygamy, I knew that the prophet had married many women. I also understood that a Muslim man has the right to have more than one wife. I was not concerned with these facts; I just accepted them. I believed that, in times past, polygamy was a normal practice. Also, other prophets married more than one woman, such as Jacob and Solomon. But two things concerned me: "Malakat Al-Yamin", and the accepted age of marriage for women as outlined in the Quran.

It states in Surah Al-Ma'arij: "Indeed, the punishment of their Lord is not that from which one is safe *And those who guard their private parts *Except from their wives or those their right hands possess, for indeed, they are not to be blamed" (Al-Ma'arij 70:28-30). These verses say you must keep your sexual purity or else you will be punished by God, unless you're sleeping with your wives or your possessions of the right hand, known as "Malakat Al-Yamin". I checked the meaning of "Malakat Al-Yamin" and learned these are female slaves. This means that Islam allows men to have female slaves and sleep with them outside of marriage. This practice is also mentioned, not once, but fourteen times in the Quran in the following Surahs: Al-Nour (3x), An-Nisa (4x), Al-Mu'minun (4x), and Al-Ahzeb (3x).

How could God allow this? Some people told me the culture and era had changed since the Quran was written. If that's true, it would be understood that polygamy was the common, acceptable practice in history. And yet, the prophet Jesus did not endorse polygamy or sleeping with female slaves. He lived more than two thousand years ago, and yet He taught a man should be married to one wife. Furthermore, the Christian men of Jesus' time married just one woman. Therefore, polygamy was not a universally accepted and practiced custom, even in the line of Islam's prophets. It is unbelievable to think that the Muslim religion—the most holy, perfect, and godly religion in the world—could allow such practices.

Regarding the accepted age of marriage for women, the following verse speaks of the time a woman should remain unmarried after divorce or being widowed:

> And those who no longer expect menstruation among your women - if you doubt, then their period is three months, and [also for] those who have not menstruated. And for those who are pregnant, their term is until they give birth. And whoever fears Allah - He will make for him of his matter ease. (Al-Talak 65:4)

As seen, the verse mentions three types of women. I checked commentaries to see who "those who have not menstruated" are. My findings showed they are young girls who haven't had their first menstruation yet. By this definition, a female child can get married, divorced, and remarry again. How could God find child marriage acceptable?

Thinking about these verses exhausted me; I spent nights without rest, searching for excuses for these dilemmas. I asked God why He did not remove such verses if they are not valid for today. For, because these verses remain in the Quran, Muslims can still use them to justify such actions, as Muslims believe that the Quran is valid regardless of the time period.

I found other injustices toward women as delineated in Islam as well. For example, when a woman enters heaven, she will be reunited with her husband, while when a man enters heaven he will receive seventy-seven virgins[17]. The following is also true of a woman as described in the Quran[18]:

- She has the right to one husband only.
- She is considered unclean during her menstruation.
- When menstruating, she does not have the right to pray or fast.
- She cannot ask for a divorce.
- Her witness is considered half of the witness of a man.
- She gets half of the heritage a man can receive.
- She is not allowed to pray out loud.

None of this is fair, and I felt pity for them.

---

[17] "Islam and Women,", *WikiIslam*, last modified June 3, 2025, https://wikiislam.net/wiki/Islam_and_Women.

[18] "Qur'an, Hadith and Scholars:Women," *WikiIslam*, last modified June 4, 2025, https://wikiislam.net/wiki/Qur%27an,_Hadith_and_Scholars:Women.

CHAPTER 6: CONFLICT OF RITUALS

"I started seeing there was a huge difference between my Muslim religion and the Christian faith."

U pon taking an appraising look at the rituals of my own religion, I found them confusing given that certain details seemed at odds with each other. For example, I looked again into "Al-Basmala" (full translation: "In the name of God, the Gracious, the Merciful"), which is written in the first verse of the Quran's first Surah (Hafs version) and above each Surah's content throughout the holy book. Before Muslims can begin reading any portion of the Quran they must say, "Al-Basmala". However, this phrase is not to be said when praying since it is not believed to have been directly transmitted to Mohamed from God; this must therefore have been a later addition to the Quran (further evidence of the Quran being altered!).

But why is it acceptable to read but not pray the same phrase? If "Al-Basmala" honors God, why is it offensive in one form of worship but not another? Also, many times the Quran is quoted during a prayer; at these times, however, a Muslim is still not to say "Al-Basmala". But then, since the Quran's verses are being spoken aloud without "Al-

Basmala", wouldn't that be offensive and make the prayers unacceptable to God? I felt torn as to whether I should pray with this phrase or not.

Another common Islamic ritual is "Al-Wudhou"[19], or ablutions: before praying, the hands must be washed three times, mouth three times, nose three times, face three times, hands again three times, hair one time, ears one time, then feet three times. This ritual is to be done in order and without interruption.

One day, while doing "Al-Wudhou", I noticed that I made a mistake. So, I went back to redo it. When I began the prayer, I remembered I had not done "Al-Nyia", or vocally declared my internal decision to perform "Al-Wudhou", and the declaration must be said before prayer. I went to rewash again, pressured by the delay. In the middle of the ritual, a verse from the Bible came to mind that I had heard on the Arabic radio station: "Come to me, all you who labour and are heavily burdened, and I will give you rest" (Matthew 11:28).

I asked myself some serious questions:

- Why is God making it so difficult to pray to Him?

---

[19] "Ablution," WikiIslam, last modified March 7, 2021, https://wikiislam.net/wiki/Ablution.

- Why are our prayers rejected when simple mistakes are made during the rituals?
- Why must the same rituals be repeated five times a day, even though they have nothing to do with what is in the heart?
- Why does He want me to be physically clean to be able to meet Him, while the biggest problem is the dirt of the heart and not the flesh? Jesus criticized the Pharisees in the Bible for cleaning themselves on the outside but not being clean on the inside (Matthew 23:25-28), calling them hypocrites and commanding that they clean the inside so the outside may also be clean!
- Why is the God of Christians asking me to come with all I have—my dirt, my mistakes, my guilt, my fear, and my sadness—yet He promises to give me rest?
- Why are all these compulsive and obligatory rituals a part of Islam to reach to God, while in Christianity God is right there and good works follow because you are loved by God and love Him in return first?

I started seeing there was a huge difference between my Muslim religion and the Christian faith.

CHAPTER 7: THE PROPHETHOOD

"I noticed several, less-than-God-honoring reasons why Mohamed might have claimed prophethood..."

A long with the rest of my studies, I wanted to understand more about the prophet himself. When I delved into the Quran and Hadiths and considered generalized beliefs of Muslims, true to the pattern I had witnessed in other areas, I found conflicting accounts and details.

The "Unlettered" Prophet

One notable area of conflict lies with the belief that Mohamed was illiterate, or unlettered. Muslims believe that Mohamed could neither read nor write; Mohamed's being given the Quran and being able to share all its content is therefore deemed a miracle of God and is proof of Mohamed's authenticity.

However, when you look within the Quran itself, it contradicts the idea of Mohamed's illiteracy. For example, the very first commandment Mohamed claimed he received from God is recorded in the first verse of the Quran: "Recite in the name of your Lord who created, Created man from a clinging substance. Recite, and your Lord is the most Generous, Who taught by the pen, Taught man that which he knew not" (Al-Alaq 96:1-5; Quick note: although the order of the Quran's chapters puts these verses at the start of Surah 96, it is considered the first content Mohamed received from God chronologically). Both the words "recite" and "read" in Arabic are "iqraa". Why would God ask Mohamed to read if he was illiterate? As per the first commandment, even if Mohamed was illiterate, he should have obeyed God and learned to read. Otherwise, he is disobeying God's first commandment.

In Hadith 6932 of Sahih Al-Bukhari, we also see evidence of Mohamed's ability to write:

> As the Prophet approached his time of death, there were men in the house. Among them was, Umar bin Al-Khattab. The Prophet said, "Come near let me write for you a writing after which you will never go astray."
>
> Umar said, "The Prophet is seriously ill, and you have the Qur'an. So, Allah's Book is sufficient for us." The people in the house differed and disputed...
>
> When they made much noise and differed greatly before the Prophet, he said to them, "Go away and leave me".
>
> Ibn-Abbas used to say, "It was a great disaster that their differences and noise

prevented Allah's Messenger from writing for them."

This anecdote clearly shows that Mohamed was able to write.

Some people will say that the Quran confirmed Mohamed was illiterate, quoting verses such as this one: "Those who follow the Messenger, the unlettered prophet, whom they find written in what they have of the Torah and the Gospel" (Al-A'raf 7:157). However, the Arabic word "الأمي" that is translated to "unlettered" here is also translated as "Gentile", meaning any non-Jew; in fact, everywhere else in the Quran where this word is found, it is interpreted as "Gentile" instead of "unlettered". Mohamed was indeed a Gentile given that he was not Jewish; therefore, it is not a strong argument to claim that the Surah Al-A'raf is stating Mohamed is illiterate when it is just as likely, or even more logical, for it to be describing him as a Gentile.

Outside Influences

As shared before, Muslims believe that all the Quran's content was completely original and given to Mohamed directly from God. And yet, aside from today's Quran having outside influences after Mohamed's death, there is also evidence that Mohamed's revelations that became the Quran's direct text were themselves influenced by other sources contemporary to Mohamed's time.

For example, in Hadith 2255 of Sahih Muslim, `Amr b. Sharid reported his father as saying this:

> One day when I rode behind Allah's Messenger, he said to me,
>
> > "Do you remember any poetry of Umayya b. Abu Salt?"
>
> > I said, "Yes." He said, "Then go on."
>
> > I recited a couplet, and he said, "Go on."
>
> > Then I again recited a couplet and he said, "Go on."
>
> > I recited one hundred couplets (of his poetry).

As seen, Mohamed was listening in this instance to the poetry of Umayya b. Abu-Salt. Abu-Salt was a poet of the Arab tribe Thaqīf who represented ideas similar to Islam and used to believe in the God of Ibrahim (Abraham) before the appearance of Islam. Abu-Salt has many poems regarding Mary and the sacrifice of Abraham that are very similar to the Quran, suggesting that Mohamed took from poetry of his day for these portions of the holy book.

Aside from poetry, it is recorded in the Hadiths that Mohamed was mentored for fifteen years by Waraqah Ibn-Nawfal, his uncle through marriage to his first wife, Khadija. If you look into the history of

Ibn-Nawfal, this man was actually a leader of the Ebionite Christians located in Mecca at that time[20]. Ebionite Christians hold to some beliefs of the Christian faith but reject others such as the doctrine of grace and the deity of Jesus. Ibn-Nawfal had much knowledge of the Christian Old and New Testaments and was even preparing Mohamed to become the next Ebionite Christian leader before his passing; because of this, Ibn-Nawfal would have taught Mohamed much of the Old and New Testament that aligns with the Ebionites' thinking. And as a result:

> When Muhammad... first announced that he was receiving revelations from God, the revelations were in large part direct copies of the stories he had heard from Waraka ibn Nawfal, as one can observe from his pattern of speaking in the Quran... as evidenced by the dramatic change in style of the portions of the Quran written after Waraka's death.[21]

Therefore, it is evident that Mohamed took from the Christian Bible in the formation of the Quran as well.

There is even indication within the Quran that Mohamed took from local legends or fables of his

---

[20] Ahmed Joktan, *From Mecca to Christ: A true story from the son of the Meccan mufti* (Washington: Proclaim Publishers, 2020), 202.

[21] See footnote 20.

time. The Quran confirms that the Arabs during Mohamed's time were not impressed by his claims to be a prophet with divine revelations; in fact, they said, "'These revelations are only' ancient fables which he has had written down, and they are rehearsed to him morning and evening'" (Al-Forqan 25:5). In another Surah, it states, "whenever Our revelations are recited to him, he says, 'Ancient fables!'" (Al-Qalam 68:15), indicating that his contemporaries had heard Mohamed's stories before he told them and considered them fairytales. This suggests that Mohamed's sources even extended to pagan material.

Motivations of Mohamed

I wondered what might have motivated Mohamed to claim to be a prophet. Muslims, of course, believe that he is indeed a prophet, and therefore was simply speaking the truth. There is, however, a significant detail missing when considering Mohamed's stated prophethood. The Quran confirms for all other Islamic prophets that they were told by God directly or by an angel of God that they were a prophet; Mohamed was never told this.

When Mohamed was in the dark cave wherein he first received revelations, at night and alone, the supernatural being never identified itself as God or an angel; there is also no report that this being informed Mohamed that Mohamed was a prophet. When Mohamed emerged from the cave, he actually believed he had been visited by a demon; it was a common belief among the Arabs of that time that "*jinn,* or magical genies, inhabited dirty, deserted places such as abandoned homes and caves."[22] Waraqah Ibn-Nawfal and Mohamed's wife Khadija were the ones to counter this and tell him he had heard from an angel of God and was a prophet. Being confirmed by man but not by God of being a prophet? This is concerning.

As I continued to study Mohamed's life in the Quran, I noticed several, less-than-God-honoring reasons why Mohamed might have claimed prophethood:

1) Money and possessions
   ◆ Al-Anfal 8:41: "And know that whatever spoils you gain, to God belongs its fifth, and to the Messenger, and the relatives, and the orphans, and the poor, and to the wayfarer..."
      o Mohamed used to take one-fifth of what they would gain in every

---

[22] Ahmed Joktan, *From Mecca to Christ: A true story from the son of the Meccan mufti* (Washington: Proclaim Publishers, 2020), 203.

major battle he started (twenty-nine battles before he died).

- Al-Anfal 8:1: "They ask you about the bounties (Anfal). Say, 'The bounties (Anfal) are for God and the Messenger.' So be mindful of God, and settle your differences, and obey God and His Messenger, if you are believers."
    - o The bounties (Anfal) refer to the portion of the spoils of war.
- Al-Hashr 59:7: "What Allah gave as booty (Fai') to His Messenger from the people of the townships—it is for Allah, His Messenger, the kindred, the orphans, the poor, and the wayfarer."
    - o Fai' is booty the Muslims acquire from the disbelievers without fighting or using cavalry and camelry in war.

It is clear that Mohamed profited financially from his status as God's Messenger—taking the bounties, the Anfal, the Fai', gifts, and from other leaders.

2) Sex and pleasure
- Al-Ahzeb 33:50: "O Prophet! We have permitted to you your wives to whom you have given their dowries, and those you already have, as granted to you by God, and

the daughters of your paternal uncle, and the daughters of your paternal aunts, and the daughters of your maternal uncle, and the daughters of your maternal aunts who emigrated with you, and a believing woman who has offered herself to the Prophet, if the Prophet desires to marry her, exclusively for you, and not for the believers. We know what We have ordained for them regarding their wives and those their right-hands possess. This is to spare you any difficulty."

- o The prophet used to have more wives than anyone else; at one time he had nine wives simultaneously and sources vary but one source claims he consummated the marriage "with thirteen women, divorced another six, and had concubines" before passing away[23]. The normal Muslim man has the right to have four wives. In addition to wives, Mohamed of course had his "Malakat Al-Yamin", or female

---

[23] "Islam and Women," https://wikiislam.net/wiki/Islam_and_Women #Muhammad_and_Women.

slaves who he would sleep with as well.

- Some Muslims try to justify Mohamed's marriages to so many women by saying the prophet did so to unify the tribes in the Arabian peninsula. If this were true...[24]
  - Why did he marry Maria the Copt, who was given to him as a gift from the Byzantine King in Egypt, Mukaokas?
  - Why did he marry Zeynab Bintu-Jahch, his adopted son's wife?
  - Why did he marry Safiya Bintu-Houyay and then *kill* her tribe?
  - Why did he marry Aisha, the daughter of his friend, Abu-Bakr, who was six years old when betrothed and nine years old when the marriage was consummated?
  - Why did he marry his friend Omar's daughter, Hafsa?

3) Power and authority
- Al-Ma'idah 92: "And obey Allah and obey the Messenger and beware. And if you turn away—then know that upon Our

---

[24] See footnote 22.

Messenger is only [the responsibility for] clear notification."

- Al-Ahzab 36: "It is not for a believing man or a believing woman, when Allah and His Messenger have decided a matter, that they should [thereafter] have any choice about their affair. And whoever disobeys Allah and His Messenger has certainly strayed into clear error."
  - o Mohamed was considered to have absolute authority second only to God himself, and therefore had to be obeyed in all matters.

When one examines the above quotes, it takes little pondering to conclude that Mohamed's motivations were earth-oriented and not God-oriented. My faith in the trustworthiness of Islam's great prophet and his portrayal as a holy man had crumbled.

CHAPTER 8: ILLUMINATED

*"Christianity has a deeper revelation about God
and His goodness."*

When I realized that all the Hebrew words and stories mentioned in the Quran were also in the Bible, it further fueled my curiosity. I yearned to understand these mysteries more deeply, thinking I might understand the Quran better if I could know what the Bible was saying.

For this reason, I purchased a Bible from a famous bookstore in Tunis. I read it from Genesis to the Apocalypse, gaining a full picture of God's plan. I had many revelations and felt illuminated. I finally understood the purpose of sending prophets in the Old Testament. I understood why people need a Savior. My conclusion after reading the Bible is that Jesus is represented in the sum of the book. Consider these:

- Adam—the first human to sin and bring death to the world (Romans 5:12-14).
- Jesus—the first human who obeyed God and brought life to the world (Romans 5:17-19).

- Noah—saved eight people from the judgment of God by building an ark (1 Peter 3:20).
- Jesus—the only Savior from the coming judgment (Acts 4:11-12).
- Abraham—offered his son as a sacrifice to God (Genesis 22; Hebrews 11:17-19).
- Jesus—the perfect sacrifice offered by God (Hebrews 10:11-14).
- Joseph—betrayed by his brothers, who then thought he was dead. But after seventeen years, they found him living as a king (Genesis 45:4-8,26).
- Jesus—crucified by the Jews, but He was resurrected on the third day as the King of Kings (Matthew 27:1-2,24-35; 1 Corinthians 15:4, 1 Timothy 6:14-15).
- Moses—the one who saved the people of God from slavery in Egypt (Exodus 3:10-12, 14:30-31).
- Jesus—the One who saves us from the slavery of sin (Galatians 5:1).
- Joshua— the one who took the people of God to the promised land (book of Joshua).
- Jesus—the One who will take us to the promised land, our eternal home with God, free of sin and judgment (John 14:3-6; Romans 6:23).

- David—the King of Israel (2 Samuel 5:3).
- Jesus—the eternal King of all (1 Timothy 6:14-15, Isaiah 9:7).
- Solomon—the one who built the temple of God (1 Kings 6:1-2).
- Jesus—the One through whom we become God's temple by the Holy Spirit (Acts 2:38, 1 Corinthians 6:19).
- Jonah—stayed in the whale's stomach until the third day (Matthew 12:40).
- Jesus—stayed in the tomb until the third day (1 Corinthians 15:4).

Jesus was the One conceived by the Holy Spirit and born of a virgin. He brought the divine nature of God to the world to show people the only true, loving God. He taught people how to live. He is the Word of God (Revelation 19:13) and gave the Spirit of God to man[25] (Acts 11:17). He is the One who knew no sin (2 Corinthians 5:21). He performed many miracles: He raised the dead, fed the hungry, gave sight to the blind, walked upon the water, and commanded the storm to be still. He taught people love and kindness. He was crucified by those He gave His life to save and asked God to forgive them.

---

[25] "13 Bible Verses about God Giving His Spirit," *Knowing Jesus*, accessed August 6, 2025, https://bible.knowing-jesus.com/topics/God-Giving-His-Spirit.

He was hurt and rejected, but He continued to show love and mercy, even to the thief who was crucified next to Him. He died and was resurrected on the third day (1 Corinthians 15:4). He ascended to heaven and promised to return to judge the world (2 Corinthians 5:10).

Specifically, when looking at Jesus' crucifixion, there are many details that support the veracity of this event. Despite the Islamic belief that Jesus was not crucified, consider the following:

- Muslims have various explanations for why Jesus was not crucified but none of them actually make sense; they cannot sufficiently argue away that this took place.
- Historical facts and documents record Jesus' crucifixion, including secular sources like the historian, Josephus.
- The first Christians and Apostles believed in the crucifixion and they shared the good news; this is what the Christian faith is all about.
- The word Enjil simply means "the good news", with salvation through the crucifixion of Jesus at its core; if Jesus was not crucified, the fundamental message of the Enjil would not be what it is.

- The prophecies of the Old Testament foretell the crucifixion of the coming Messiah (i.e., Psalm 22, Isaiah 53, etc.). These same prophecies are read by the Jews in their sacred writings, who do not even have faith in Jesus and therefore would not be trying to support the idea of Jesus' crucifixion.
- There are at least 20,000 handwritten copies of the Christian Bible's New Testament.[26]
- The Quran even mentions that Jesus was dead and then went to heaven: "And peace is on me the day I was born and the day I will die and the day I am raised alive" (Maryam 19:33).

What Mohamed did was a reconstruction of the Old Testament with certain, key parts removed. He took away freedom in the Holy Spirit, forcing people to live in slavery under laws and commandments. He removed the relationship between a Father and Son, changing it to a relationship between a master and a slave.

---

[26] Daniel B. Wallace, "The Reliability of the New Testament Manuscripts," in *The ESV Study Bible*, eds. Lane T. Dennis, Wayne Grudem, J. I. Packer, & Justin Taylor (Illinois: Crossway, 2008), 2587.

After reading the entire Bible and meditating on the teachings of Jesus, it was clear that God did not have to send any other prophet after Jesus. Jesus' teachings are enough to make us live in love and unity. Mohamed brought nothing special or new; Christianity has a deeper revelation about God, His goodness, love, tolerance, compassion, forgiveness, faith, peace, joy, and the spiritual realm.

At the age of eighteen, my life changed forever. The research, the revelations, and the many tears I had cried all added up. I had begged God to show me the truth. As a result, I had only one choice left: to accept Christ as my Lord and Savior.

Letting go of everything I ever knew was the hardest decision I ever made, but I could not resist the voice deep inside giving me joy and peace. I had never heard of anyone who had changed their religion and had no idea what the next step would be: what should I do, where should I go? My future was unknown, but I was ready to trade what I had before with the supernatural peace that was now in my heart, a heart reveling in the truth. So, I closed my eyes and said, "Thank You, Jesus, for what You have done for me. Thank You for showing me the love of God and His Fatherhood." And I surrendered my life to Jesus, the Christ.

CHAPTER 9: PERSECUTION & THE VIOLENCE OF ISLAM

"Persecution against Christians continued to worsen and it became difficult to even walk the streets alone."

S oon after my decision to follow Jesus, I was walking in the capital city when I came across a beautiful old church. Without thinking, I knocked on the door. A man opened it; he was smiling. "Come in. You're welcome here," he said.

I entered, a bit shy and nervous. I found seven people gathered around a table. Each person had a Bible like mine. They asked me to introduce myself, and I told them my story. The people praised God and prayed with me. As they sang praises, I was so overwhelmed that I could not stop crying for the remainder of the day.

I decided to become an "evangelism machine-gun"; wherever I went, I would talk about Jesus. I talked about Him while I was at home; in school; at coffee shops; with my friends, my colleagues, my band, and, frankly, anyone that I happened to meet.

But my family believed that I had become a source of trouble and a danger for them. Because of this, I was kicked out of my house. My friends did not want to talk to me anymore and began inventing stories and lies about me. Even my girlfriend left me because of my faith in Jesus.

It was deeply painful seeing everyone I had known leave my life. But thankfully, God gave me new friends and a family who believed in Christ like I did. Some were believers when I met them, and God blessed me by using me to bring others to faith through sharing of the good news. I went from being alone to becoming part of a family of twelve.

Still, persecution against Christians continued to worsen and it became difficult to even walk the streets alone. We therefore decided to move to the capital city, where greater religious tolerance presided. We continued to share our faith, and we were blessed to see our underground church grow.

And then, two years later, the revolution in Tunisia took place; the Arab Spring[27,28,29] had begun. The radical Muslims imprisoned by President Ben Ali had been set free. These radicals began manipulating people and pressuring them to turn back to Islam. The violence increased, even to the

[27] "Arab Spring," *Britannica*, accessed August 6, 2025, https://www.britannica.com/event/Arab-Spring.

[28] Ahmed Al-Jarallah, "Brotherhood starts and ends in Tunisia," *Arab Times*, last modified January 21, 2021, https://www.arabtimesonline.com/news/brotherhood-starts-and-ends-in-tunisia/.

[29] Ben Cohen and Ahmad Sharawi, "10 Things to Know About the Muslim Brotherhood," *Foundation for Defense of Democracies*, last modified June 9, 2025, https://www.fdd.org/analysis/2025/06/09/10-things-to-know-about-the-muslim-brotherhood/.

point of assassinating politicians who were against them. The president fled for his own protection to Saudi Arabia, the Muslim Brotherhood took control, and greater Islamic rule was thereafter enforced.

Some of the radicals left Tunisia to join ISIS while others remained in my country; every so often they would commit a terrorist attack, justifying their evildoing with verses from the Quran and Hadiths.

Now, please indulge me once more; in like manner to my research in the other areas of Islam, when I was seeking truth I found quote upon quote from the Quran and Hadiths (Sahih Al-Bukhari and Sahih Muslim in particular) speaking to the violence that all who truly adhere to Islam must follow to supposedly please God:

- At-Tawbah 9:29: "Fight those who do not believe in Allah or in the Last Day and who do not consider unlawful what Allah and His Messenger have made unlawful and who do not adopt the religion of truth from those who were given the Scripture - [fight] until they give the jizyah willingly while they are humbled."

- At-Tawbah 9:5: "And when the sacred months have passed, then kill the polytheists wherever you find them and capture them and besiege them and sit in wait for them at every place of ambush. But if they should repent, establish prayer, and give zakah, let them [go] on their way. Indeed, Allah is Forgiving and Merciful."

- At-Tawbah 9:14: "Fight them; Allah will punish them by your hands and will disgrace them and give you victory over them and satisfy the breasts of a believing people."

- At-Tawbah 9:123: "O you who have believed, fight those adjacent to you of the disbelievers and let them find in you harshness. And know that Allah is with the righteous."

- Al-Baqarah 2:193: "Fight them until there is no [more] fitnah and [until] worship is [acknowledged to be] for Allah. But if they cease, then there is to be no aggression except against the oppressors."

- Muhammad 47:4: "So when you meet those who disbelieve [in battle], strike [their] necks until, when you have inflicted slaughter upon them, then secure their bonds, and either [confer] favor afterwards or ransom [them] until the war lays down its burdens. That [is the command]. And if Allah had willed, He could have taken vengeance upon them [Himself], but [He ordered armed struggle] to test some of you by means of others. And those who are killed in the cause of Allah—never will He waste their deeds."

* Al-Anfal 8:60: "And prepare against them whatever you are able of power and of steeds of war by which you may terrify the enemy of Allah and your enemy and others besides them whom you do not know [but] whom Allah knows. And whatever you spend in the cause of Allah will be fully repaid to you, and you will not be wronged."

* Al-Anfal 65: "O Prophet, urge the believers to battle. If there are among you twenty [who are] steadfast, they will overcome two hundred. And if there are among you one hundred [who are] steadfast, they will overcome a thousand of those who have disbelieved because they are a people who do not understand."

* Hadith 1076 of Sahih Al-Bukhari and Sahih Muslim: "I have been commanded to fight against the people till they testify La ilaha illAllah (there is no true god except Allah) and that Muhammad is His slave and Messenger, and to establish As-Salat (Iqamat-as-Salat), and to pay Zakat; and if

they do this, then their blood and property are secured except by the rights of Islam, and their accountability is left to Allah."

And yet, despite all these verses of fighting and killing, the Quran is coinhabited by many verses that speak of peace and tolerance as well, believed to be spoken by Mohamed when he was in Mecca, such as the following:

- Al-Kafirun 109:6: "For you is your religion, and for me is my religion."
- Al-Kahf 18:29: "And say, 'The truth is from your Lord, so whoever wills—let him believe; and whoever wills—let him disbelieve.'"
- Al-Baqara 2:224: "[Believers], do not allow your oaths in God's name to hinder you from doing good, being mindful of God and making peace between people. God hears and knows everything".
- An-Nahl 16:125: "[Prophet], call [people] to the way of your Lord with wisdom and good teaching. Argue with them in the most courteous way, for your Lord knows best who has strayed from His way and who is rightly guided."

This pairing of violence and peace is yet another set of self-contradicting beliefs within Islam.

Muslims justify this contradiction by saying it is because of the "Doctrine of Abrogation", or "An-Nasakh Wa Al-Mansukh", meaning that God would send new verses in the Quran to replace the previous ones: "We do not abrogate a verse or cause it to be forgotten except that We bring forth [one] better than it or similar to it" (Al-Baqarah 2:106). And yet, we know that God does not change (Malachi 3:6 and James 1:17). And indeed, if a person says one thing is true and then later claims that same thing is false or claims the opposite is true, then he is a liar and therefore should not be trusted. Applying this definition, Mohamed has even less credibility and is, in fact, a deceiver.

Mohamed shifted from an outlook of peace to violence after his mentor Ibn-Nawfal died and after many around him rejected his claim to be a prophet of God; for a detailed history of Mohamed's life and this shift in his doctrine that translated to his Quranic statements, read my co-author Dr. Ahmed Joktan's first appendix in "From Mecca to Christ". We see deeds as well as words change when Mohamed shifted to this perspective of hate and aggression: the Hijri calendar, which is the Islamic calendar that began in the year that Mohamed fled from Mecca to Medina, has been stained with blood since its inception.

There are some Muslims who believe ISIS, terrorists, and terrorist attacks are in fact an American and Israeli conspiracy to destroy Islam[30]. However, this is clearly incorrect when one looks at the history of the Hijri calendar. America was only discovered in the year 898 of the Islamic calendar[31], while starting from the Hijri's first year, the history of Islam has been drenched in blood from Muslims both killing infidels as well as other Muslims. Indeed, the Hijri calendar accounts for the slaughter of many Muslims as well as desecrations of Islamic holy places, with some examples seen here:

- The second Khalifa, Omar Ibn Al-Khattab, was killed by a Muslim believer.
- The third Khalifa, Othman Ibn-Affan, was killed by Muslims.
- The fourth Khalifa, the cousin of the prophet Mohamed and the husband of his daughter, Ali Ibn-Abi-Taleb, was killed by Muslims.

---

[30] "History of Islamic Thought", *WikiIslam*, last modified January 26, 2023, https://wikiislam.net/wiki/History_of_Islamic_Thought.

[31] Justin Worland, "President Obama Is Not the 'Founder of ISIS.' Here's Who Really Started It", *Time*, Last modified August 11, 2016, https://time.com/4448218/donald-trump-isis-founder-president-obama-zarqawi/.

- The sons of Ali Ibn-Abi-Taleb and the grandchildren of the prophet Mohamed, Al-Hassan and Al-Hussain, were killed by Muslims, one beheaded and the other poisoned[32].

- Talha and Zoubeir, two of the ten who were given glad tidings of Paradise, were killed by Muslims[33].

- Battle of the Camel[34]: Ten thousand Muslims were killed by Muslims due to "Waqia'at Al-Jamal", a conflict between Aisha (the prophet's wife) and Ali Ibn-Abi-Taleb (the prophet's cousin).

- Battle of Saffin[35]: Seventy thousand Muslims were killed when the Muslim army of Ali Ibn-Abi-Taleb fought against the Muslim army of Muawiyah Ibn-Abi-Sufien (the first Khalifa of the dynasty of the Umayyads).

---

[32] Mohammad Redha, *Al-Hasan and al-Hussein: The two grandsons of the messenger of Allah*, trans. Mohammad Agha (Dar al-Kotob al-Ilmiyah, 1999), https://kutub.nur.nu/English/Muhammad-Rida_alHasan-wa-alHussein-eng.pdf.

[33] Discovering Islam Team, "10 Companions Were Promised Paradise – Who Are They?" *AboutIslam*, last modified August 12, 2023, https://aboutislam.net/reading-islam/about-muhammad/10-companions-were-promised-paradise-who-are-they/.

[34] Zahra Ashfaq, "Battle of Camel: Summary, who won, full story," *The Islamic Information*, last modified December 6, 2023, https://theislamicinformation.com/stories/battle-of-camel/.

[35] "Battle of Ṣiffīn: Islamic history," *Britannica*, last modified July 8, 2025, https://www.britannica.com/event/Battle-of-Siffin.

- Battle of Karbala[36]: seventy-three of the prophet's relatives were killed in a fight between Al-Hussain (the prophet's grandson) and Al-Yazid (the son of the Khalifa Muawiyah). After the death of Al-Hussain, around seven hundred were killed by the Umayyad army.

- Abdullah Ibn-Zoubayr[37], (the grandson of Al-Khalifa Abu-Bakr), was killed by Muslims.

- Marwan Ibn Al-Hakam, Omar Ibn-Abd Al-Aziz, Ibrahim Ibn Al-Walid, Abu Al-Abbas, Marwan II, Mohamed Al-Mahdi Billah, Al-Mustai'in Billah, and Mohamed Al-Mustakfi Billah were Khalifas killed by Muslims[38].

- Al-Houssayn Ibn-Noumayr[39] was a Muslim leader who destroyed the Kaaba using a catapult.

- For three days, the leader of Yazid Ibn-Muawiyah's[40] army made the Prophet's Mosque a stable.

---

[36] Meir Litvak, "Karbala," *Encyclopaedia Iranica*, last modified November 1, 2012, https://www.iranicaonline.org/articles/karbala/.

[37] "Abd Allāh ibn al-Zubayr: Companion of Muḥammad," *Britannica*, last modified October 28, 2024, https://www.britannica.com/topic/Umayyad-dynasty-Islamic-history.

[38] "Khilafah (Caliphate)," *WikiIslam*, last modified May 24, 2021, https://wikiislam.net/wiki/Khilafah_(Caliphate).

[39] "Husayn ibn Numayr al-Sakuni," *wikiwand*, last modified April 25, 2021, https://www.wikiwand.com/en/articles/Husayn%20ibn%20Numayr.

[40] "Yazīd I: Umayyad caliph," *Britannica*, last modified January 1, 2025, https://www.britannica.com/biography/Yazid-I.

In conclusion after all my research, it is clear that Islam is a religion of darkness, destruction, deception, and death. Only in Christ can we have light, illumination, liberty, and life!

* * *

Sorrowfully in my country, the pattern of violent Islamic perpetrations has continued. While many of my Christian family reside to this day in Tunisia, a few of us have left to seek safe haven, though through God's loving provision no one has been killed. As an outspoken evangelist, I personally was targeted by the new regime in Tunisia, and so I fled my home country to seek asylum in Malta. I have since been granted this safety and now am on the path to become a Maltese citizen. Wherever I am, I will proclaim Jesus' name and live my life for Him.

THE INVITATION

"Open your heart..."

On my journey from Tunisia to Christ, I had to overcome many challenges. I was raised in a religion that taught me how to obey laws and practice rituals to go to heaven and avoid eternity in hell. What I have learned throughout this journey is that God is our paradise, our heaven, and our reward. Heaven is not a place where we are going to spend our eternity drinking wine and sleeping with virgins. Heaven is God's presence, and you cannot spend eternity with God unless you begin a relationship with Him on earth. Belonging to a religion will not rescue us from spending eternity in hell. Our deeds are not able to take us to God. The only way is by being in a relationship with Jesus.

Jesus Christ was the image of God on earth. He showed us the true, loving God. Jesus is the very image of how a person's relationship should be with the Heavenly Father. Believing in Jesus is not believing in a religion or converting to a new belief. Believing in Jesus means that you accept the fact you are not able to reach God through your good deeds; you ask God to come into your life and change you instead. Then your good deeds will be a result of your relationship with God and the manifestation of the Holy Spirit, who will live in you.

Believing in Jesus means we believe that God is just, that we were separated from God because of the disobedience of one human being (Adam), and that the righteousness of one human being (Jesus) can take us back to His presence. As God gave Adam and Eve free will to choose His presence in their lives or to eat from the forbidden tree in Eden, He is now giving you the free will to choose His salvation through Jesus Christ, who is the way, the truth, and the life.

So, I invite you, dear reader, to accept today the free gift of salvation through the Savior Jesus Christ. Open your heart and ask God to come and fill it with His presence. "Today if you will hear his voice, don't harden your hearts" (Hebrews 3:15).

You may obtain this and many other fine
resources made available by
Proclaim Publishers by contacting us:

Web: proclaimpublishers.com

Email: info@proclaimpublishers.com

Postal Mail:
1317 Edgewater Drive, Suite 4774
Orlando, FL, 32804

SOLI DEO GLORIA